FUTURE OF SOCIAL MEDIA & METAVERSE

IN THIS BOOK MENTIONS ALL SOCIAL MEDIA MARKETING TECHNOLOGY AND TRENDS.

KP PANCHAL

ISBN 979-888606775-0

Contents

Author Note

Hello Friends I'm Kp panchal Digital entrepreneur and Social media consultant. I want To share some topics on Social Media Marketing in This Book. My social media Journey started in 2015. and I'm Learn All things in Social media marketing from Time to time and upgrading yourself. Social media strategy and Technology change every Day so you also know about Social media marketing Future in this Book I mentioned all Social media trends and Future Technology. If you Want you are Run Successful Business in 2022 so this is Book for you.

Do you want to Grow your Business Online in 2022 -2025?

How to generate Revenue and Retain your Customer with New Social media Trends

This book Mentions all Social media marketing technology and Trends. I hope you Read, Enjoy and Grow your Business, Thanks

Preface

Social Network Usage & Growth Statistics:

How Many People Use Social Media in 2022

Social Media Usage Statistics (Top Picks)

4.48 billion people currently use social media worldwide, up more than double from 2.07 billion in 2015

The average social media user engages with **an average of 6.6 various social media platforms**

The social media growth rate since 2015 is an average of **12.5%** year-over-year. However, growth is on the decline with 2019-2020 data revealing a **9.2%** growth rate

By region, social media growth in 2019-2020 is led by Asia: **+16.98%**, Africa **+13.92%**, South America **+8.00%**, North America **+6.96%**, Europe **+4.32%**, and Australasia **+4.9%**

60.99% of the 7.87 billion people in the world use social media, of eligible audiences aged 13+, there is **63%** that are active users

93.33% of internet users are on social media; however, a titanic **85%** of mobile internet users are active on networks

Out of **4.48 billion** social media users, **99%** access websites or apps through a mobile device, with only **1.32%** accessing platforms exclusively via desktop

Globally, the **average time** a person spends on social media a day is **2 hours 24 minutes**; if someone signed up at 16 and lived to 70, they would spend **5.7 years** of their life on it

Facebook is the leading social network at **2.9 billion** monthly active users, followed by YouTube **(2.3 billion)**, WhatsApp **(2 billion)**, FB Messenger **(1.3 billion)**, and WeChat **(1.2 billion)**

72.3% of the total US population actively use social media, totaling several **240 million** people

In the US, **54%** of social media users are female, while the remaining 46% are male, compared with a global average of 45.6% for females, and 54.4% for males.

How many people use social media?

As of 2021, the number of people using social media is over 4.48 billion worldwide, with the average user accessing 6.6 social media platforms monthly. Popular platforms like Facebook have over 65.86% of their monthly users logging in to use social media daily.

All social networks report growth data on the number of monthly active users or MAUs rather than the number of accounts, as this data is more accurate for measuring actual use and territory penetration.

What percentage of people use social media?

The current percentage of people using social media is 56.8% of the world's total population. However, when we look into platform penetration rates from people in eligible audiences, 93.33% of 4.8 billion global internet users and 85% of 5.27 billion mobile phone users are on social media.

4.48 billion people use social media worldwide, according to platform reports on the current number of active users

56.8% of the world's population is active on social media when looking at eligible audiences aged 13+ years, rising to 82% in North America

Out of **7.87** billion people in the world, **56.8%** of the population use social networks, regardless of age or internet access

Out of **4.8** billion internet users, **93.33%** are active users

Out of **5.27** billion unique mobile phone users, **85%** are active users

Out of **4.48** billion social media users, **99%** access the websites or apps through a mobile device

How many social media accounts does the average person have?

According to the Global Web Index, the average number of social media accounts a millennial or Gen Z-er has is 8.4 worldwide, up 75% from 4.8 accounts in 2014. The study of 46 countries with internet users aged 16 to 64 shows Japan had the lowest average number of social network accounts at 3.8, comparably India had the highest with 11.5 per person.

The average number of social media accounts is **8.4 per person** in 2020

The growth in the number of accounts per person is up **75%** from **4.8 accounts per person in 2014 to 8.4 in 2020**

Firstly, the growth of multi-networking relates to the widening of **platform choice**. Secondly, it's also down to

specialization of individual platforms, e.g., Instagram (photos), YouTube (video), and LinkedIn (work)

5 Highlights for Backlinko's audience:

India: Averages **11.4** accounts per person

USA: Averages **7.1** accounts per person

UK: Averages **6.9** accounts per person

Canada: Averages **6.8** accounts per person

Japan: Averages **3.8** accounts per person

How many people use social networks for business?

40% of all internet users worldwide use social media for work purposes. In the U.S., only 27% of people actively use social media in their jobs, compared with the highest by country in Indonesia at 65%, or the lowest at 13% in Israel.

5 Highlights for Backlinko's audience:

India:47% of people use it for work

Canada:31% of people use it for work

Australia:30% of people use it for work

USA:27% of people use it for work

UK:27% of people use it for work

Which gender uses social media more by region?

North America:54% female vs. **46%** male users

South America:52% female vs. **48%** male users

Western Europe:50% female vs. **50%** male users

Southern Africa:52% female vs. **48%** male users

Southern Asia:27% female vs. **73%** male users

Oceania:53% female vs. **47%** male users

Which gender uses social media more by platform?

As you can see from the data above, social network usage is different for men and women globally when examining location. Perhaps the most notable gap in gender differences is where we look at the use by the platform. When looking at the top 8 social platforms by monthly active users, YouTube, LinkedIn, Twitter, and TikTok index higher in male users. Sites like Facebook and Instagram are more female orientated, especially Pinterest, which dominates with the female audience

Global social media growth rates

How much does social networking grow year on year?

In 2021, there are 4.48 billion people actively using social media in the world, and this is an increase of 13.13% year-on-year from 3.69 billion in 2020. Back in 2015, there were only 2.07 billion users – that's an overall increase in users of 115.59% in just six years.

6 Year Social Media Growth Statistics:

2021: 4.480 billion active users **(+13.13%)**

2020: 3.960 billion active users **(+13.7%)**

2019: 3.484 billion active users **(+9.2%)**

2018: 3.196 billion active users **(+9.0%)**

2017: 2.796 billion active users **(+21%)**

2016: 2.307 billion active users **(+11%)**

2015: 2.078 billion active users

Top 10: Growth of social media users by country

According to Keipo's analysis, the country with the most significant social media growth in 2019-2020 was India, with 130 million new users joining platforms – equivalent to 9.6% of their total population. In second place was China (15 m), Indonesia (12 m), Brazil (11 m), Iran (9.4 m), and the USA in 6th place with 6.9 million new users.

Below, we have the top 20 social media growth rankings by country, representing the largest number of users, not percentage increase:

Growth of social media users by region

The total number of people using social media grew by 9.2% between April 2019 and Jan 2020. When looking at the number of people growing by region, Europe had the slowest activation of new active users at 4.9%. Whereas Asia was the most considerable social media user base growth at 16.98%, followed by Africa increasing by 13.92%

Social media growth by region 2019-2020:

North America: +6.96%

South America: +8.00%

Europe: +4.32%

Africa: +13.92%

Asia: +16.98%

Australasia: +4.9%

Day one: When did social media start?

The rise of social media began back in 1996 with the release of the networking site Bolt (now closed). Shortly after, in 1997, Six Degrees was released where users could add friends and make profiles. Following that, services like AOL Instant Messenger, Live Journal, and Friendster launched all paving the way for the leader, Facebook, in

2004.

Timeline: Early days of social media

1996: The first social networking and video website is Bolt, which was active from 1996-to 2007

1997: A site called Six Degrees was created where users could upload profile information and connect with users by making 'friends'

1997: AOL launched its Instant Messenger service, which acquired it from an Israeli based company, it was originally called ICQ and launched in 1996

1999: This was the launch of LiveJournal, the first popular blogging platform

2000: Habbo, a game based networking site, was released

2002: Friendster launched, where users made profiles, connected, and share content

2003: LinkedIn launched the first business-orientated social networking site

2004: Facebook, the most popular platform of all time launches

Sources: GlobalWebIndex, Pew Research, Wikipedia, Social media platforms & Kepio's Analysis

Social media penetration by country

Which country has the most active social media users in the world?

Social media penetration = active users vs. total population.

According to Statista's data from 2020, the most active country is the U.A.E., with 99% of its population using social media. The average penetration rate globally is 49%. When isolating the data to eligible users aged 13+, the average social media penetration rate is 63%.

Key Statistics by the total population

On average, **49%** of the world are active social media users, regardless of age

On average, **63%** of the world's population aged 13+ are active on social media

The USA has **70%** regardless of age, **83%** for only those aged 13+ years

The UK has **66%** regardless of age, **79%** for only those aged 13+ years

Canada has **67%** regardless of age, **77%** for only those aged 13+ years

Australia has **71%** regardless of age, **85%** for only those aged 13+ years

India has **29%** regardless of age, **38%** for only those aged 13+ years

In which countries can networks look to expand?

Social media has the most substantial opportunity for growth in developing countries, with billions of new users to sign up. Think tank data company Pew Research Center noted a steady increase in internet and smartphone adoption, which significantly relates to the growth of social media in certain developing countries or regions.

In 2014 there was a median of 42% of people that accessed the internet occasionally, now this figure must be well over 65%, which was the last number recorded from the Pew study in 2017. There was a similar story for the adoption of smartphone use also, doubling to almost 42% in the same period.

Advertising revenue will not grow at the same rate

Unfortunately, social networks looking to expand in these territories will make a lot less from the advertising profits per user, so user volume is critical for their earnings.

For example, Facebook reports the average revenue per user would be $41.41 for signing someone up in the US; however, in the Asia-Pacific region, that figure lies at $3.57.

Social media in the US by the numbers

What percentage of Americans are on social media?

According to platform statements, the number of social media users in the US is 240 million in 2020, meaning 72.3% of Americans are actively using sites monthly. The most popular platforms in the United States are YouTube at 81.9% and Facebook at 73.4% among internet users aged 16 to 64.

CHAPTER ONE

INFLUENCER MARKETING

Influencer marketing has become popular on social media very quickly. It has even beaten print marketing in terms of popularity on Google Trends. People with thousands of followers can leverage their social media presence and collaborate with brands.

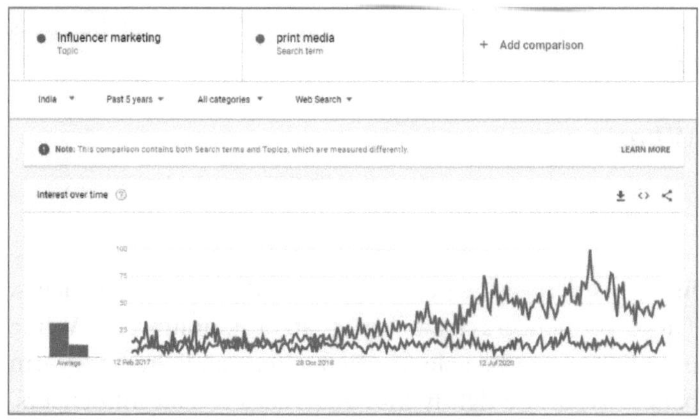

Image via Google Trends

Influencers get paid by the brands to promote their products to their audiences. Brands, on the other hand, are looking for reliable influencers to collaborate with to reach their target customers.

However, it's not only the influencers with massive fan-followings who can reap the benefits of influencer marketing on social media. As its popularity soars, big influencers are becoming expensive for SMEs.

So, what can small businesses do?

Micro-influencers have fewer followers than big influencers but they have the advantage of higher engagement among their audiences on social media. Additionally, they charge significantly less than popular influencers for their sponsored content. This makes it affordable for SMEs to collaborate with micro-influencers and promote their brands to their audiences for business growth.

What's more?

Just like micro-influencers, there are also nano-influencers. These influencers have less than 10k followers. While brands may not be able to reach a huge audience, they can benefit from the tightly-knit audiences of nan-influencers. And it doesn't require a large budget to collaborate with these smaller influencers on social media platforms.

As they may just be setting out on their influencer marketing journeys, they may seek a stable partnership. It could be a great starting point to form a long-term partnership with such social media influencers.

However, finding reliable social media influencers can be quite a challenge given the number of fake accounts on social media. You need to thoroughly analyze each social media profile and their social

media usage to figure out if it's genuine or not.

So, what can you do to make this process quicker?

To avoid this issue, you can use influencer discovery platforms. They can make the entire process of finding an influencer extremely simple.

It has a database of over 750K social media influencers and you can search for them based on hashtags, username, location, engagement rates, niche, and more.

After brands and advertisers slashed their marketing budgets for traditional mediums in 2020, digital marketing took the center stage. Within the hemisphere of digital marketing, social media became a leading channel that drove brand discovery and purchases decisions last year. Influencer marketing also got its due recognition as brands looked for affordable and niche options to reach out to GenZ and Millennials. Marketers also realized that the influencer marketing model is well-suited in a time in which the audience is looking for some inspiration to keep going on, searching DIY videos as they turned home chefs, learning new recipes, or focusing on self-care. Creators played an integral role in building a sense of community -- something people searched for when living in isolation.

Bolstered by prolonged stay-at-home periods, consumers also steered away from pictures and text and started consuming more videos than ever before. According to Bain and Company, the online video user base in India has increased to more than 350 million people, growing 24% in the last three years. Today, Indian smartphone users spend about 4.8 hours on their devices daily, of which a staggering one hour on average is spent consuming videos, said the report.

So, as video consumption scales and attention span reduces every day, influencer marketing offers quick turnaround time and personalization. Another key factor that attracted brands to this medium is the bond of trust and the authenticity that creators share with their fans, allowing brands to reach out to a niche audience.

As a result, the influencer marketing industry has gone through a severe transformation in a short time, becoming a mainstream marketing vehicle.

Brands have started looking for agencies that can provide them with interesting campaign ideas rather than just a list of influencers and expected reach. They are more involved in their marketing campaigns and have started exploring creative ideas collectively with the influencers to create engaging content. So, in 2021, we saw brands moving away from ‘one-time associations’ for single posts to collaborating with influencers for long-time deals. GroupM and INCA’s study conducted earlier this year also proves how significant influencer marketing is to a marketer today. It said that influencer marketing has become a top priority for marketers this year, as every other leader indicated a budget growth of more than 25% in 2021. INCA's report further went on to predict that the Influencer Marketing industry is poised to grow at a CAGR of 25% for the next decade, reaching a size of Rs 2200 crore in 2025. As per the report, celebrities corner only 27% of the marketing dollars while a bulk of 73% is taken by digital influencers.Keeping in mind how 2020 and its aftermath in 2021 revolutionized the digital industry, we reached out to a few influencer marketing agencies to understand what does the future hold and how is the ecosystem shaping up. Here is what they said:

Neel Gogia, Co-founder of IPLIX Media:

The upcoming year is bringing a plethora of opportunities for existing as well as aspiring influencers and creators. The first and foremost are long-term partnerships. With each passing day, more and more brands are realizing that ROI delivered by influencer marketing is unparalleled. Therefore, they are increasingly investing in influencer marketing, and especially in long-term partnerships. Long-term partnerships help them build advocates and ultimately, increase trust amongst the audience.

Apart from that, the regionalization of content will increasingly be gaining momentum in the upcoming years. In fact, global brands and platforms are already experimenting with it. Recently, LinkedIn launched its regional version after almost every major global networking app available in the country across Facebook, Twitter and Clubhouse have already introduced it to support the multiple Indian languages. In this wave of regionalization, the local languages that are gaining popularity are Telugu, Marathi, Bengali, Punjabi, Malayalam, etc.

Dharika Merchant, COO, WORD and Alchemy Group:

The influencer marketing industry in 2022 will see a huge rise in the demand for micro-influencers.

Micro influencers‘ share in the total industry increased drastically last year due to brands favoring them owing to their higher engagement rates & affordability. The industry is expected to shift to a more data-driven approach which will become the primary reason for the rise in demand for micro-influencers. Brands are now willing to work on branded content with micro-influencers due to favorable data and better insights. It also leads to an effortless long-term relationship between the brand and the influencer thereby ensuring an always-on marketing approach. This always-on influencer marketing approach portrays brand loyalty from an influencer point of view and adds to the credibility of the brand and better brand recall. without a doubt, focusing on micro-influencers will be one of the leading trends for the industry in the coming year and we're excited to see how this changes the face of branded content.

'Live streaming' is all set to emerge as one of the widely accepted and used influencer marketing tools in the coming year. Live-eCommerce as a concept was started in China last year during the pandemic and got popularized amongst other nations. Live-eCommerce is a great way to connect with the right set of target audiences and turn them into 'customers' of the brand the influencers are vouching for. This is one of the best ways for brands who are focusing on 'ROI' driven campaigns and not on awareness or brand-building. In India, with many start-ups and MSME brands now focusing on performance-driven influencer marketing campaigns, the concept of live-eCommerce will be practiced and this shall disrupt the influencer marketing industry.

Brands promoting highly accessible and affordable products and services are more likely to make use of this new concept. Alongside, live streaming is known for enabling better connections between creators, brands, and consumers as it is a more authentic and real-time content piece. It also provides an opportunity for consumers to interact with their favorite creators, thereby there is a larger scope for personalization, feedback, and results-driven conversations. Currently, the live-streaming concept is highly dominated by gamers, and this trend will soon see a shift. The live-stream feature provides an equal opportunity and benefits to influencers and content creators of all kinds if used strategically and creatively. For eg: Content creator, Viya from China live-streams about beauty, cosmetics, real estate, cars, and rockets; and is gaining immense out of such brand deals. Likewise, we too are soon to witness such a trend in India.

Apaksh Gupta, CEO, and Founder, One Impression:

While there are going to be plenty of emerging trends that we are expecting to take over the influencer marketing economy in 2022, one particular trend that is going to stand out is the mainstreaming of the metaverse. The way the world of content and social media is evolving, we can easily assume now that the metaverse is here. While the pandemic forced brands to jump on the digital marketing train, newer technological innovation and integration of various platforms to build a virtual ecosystem is bringing the dream of Metaverse closer every day.

2022 is going to witness a lot of investments from brands into mainstreaming the metaverse. We have already seen in 2021 that bigger brands like Nike and Verizon are already initiating their strategies to get a head start in this league from their competitors. Gucci has also launched its limited collection for Roblox letting players customize their avatars in Gucci products. In 2022, we will be witnessing an increase in these numbers of brands that will be deploying technologies like AR/VR with influencers and content creators at the center of them to promote their products and services.

Rohan Tyagi, VP Strategy and Operations, India - Triller:

The advent of technologies like NFTs, Crypto has opened up new engagement and revenue channels for brands. In fact, there is great affinity toward it among GenZ and millennial buyers. Through NFTs, brands can disrupt their markets with new strategies to raise awareness, develop new consumer journeys and increase customer value and loyalty. However, In the decentralized world of Web3, the power has shifted back to creators, and brands looking to leverage technologies like NFTs know that they cant simply buy into the space. Community interest today is driven by creators as a result, there will be an uptick in brands partnering with influencers to leverage the opportunities afforded by NFTs.

While influencer marketing is a fairly young industry with Metaverse becoming mainstream there is a huge likelihood of it taking off quickly and becoming a multibillion-dollar economy in the virtual world. In fact, this may happen much quicker than we think.

Aayush Tiwari, VP - Talent Management & Music Business, Monk Entertainment:

One pretty evident trend is the dominance of short video content. We've noticed a wave of crisp crunchable 15-30 seconder bites taking the internet by storm in 2021 already, bound to multiply in the coming years. Factors that act as a catalyst are low entry barrier, easy to make, large-scale consumption. What drives the short video ecosystem is the ability of it get recreated under the banner of 'trends.' Every week, there are hypothetically ten new trends which garner lakhs of videos lifting the consumption and UGC levels to higher levels. Dominant social media platforms like Instagram, YouTube launched their verticals, and new players like MOJ, TakaTak, Chingari entered the game encouraging regional tiers to showcase their talent. Even Netflix launched a short vertical that features the best scenes from their series, which people are bingeing on the go.

Vaibhav Odhekar, Managing director India & Middle East, AnyMind Group:

Influencer marketing has seen few major changes from the consumer approach towards the whole marketing and influencer segment and monetization of platforms. With the rising social media consumption and engagement, D2C brands across segments have moved towards influencers marketing. As per the 'State of Influencer in Asia 2021' report by Antag, the most popular are Art & Entertainment, Food & Beverage, and Fashion & Beauty while Finance, health & wellness are also attractive eyeballs and set to become trendsetting in 2022.

One of the trends that stood out this year was Influencers creating and launching their own brands, driven by their expertise in a certain field, passion, or life experience. Along with Direct-to-consumer and e-commerce, Consumer behavior shifts driven by the pandemic have accelerated trends. We've also noticed a trend of rising social commerce which will stay. Platforms like Facebook, Instagram, YouTube and Twitter have already made such features available in some parts of the world. The report also found out that Youtube is the most used social media platform in India. As we move towards 2022, more trends will see a spike and the ongoing trends will keep growing with the brands' demand.

Sagar Pushp, Co-founder and CEO, ClanConnect:

Two major trends are emerging in the influencer marketing sector and will likely dominate in 2022. Firstly, the creator economy will move towards a subscription-led model wherein true fans will be able to pay a sum of money to access exclusive influencer content. Such premium content will not be available on public platforms like Instagram and YouTube. Secondly, the use of NFTs is going to skyrocket over the next year. With NFTs, users can assume ownership of content such as images, videos, or sound clips, unlocking more revenue opportunities for creators.

Pulkit Agrawal, Co-Founder & CEO, Trell:

Two words: Social Commerce. While the pandemic has given a massive push to India's creator economy, the industry will thrive in 2022, with newer shopping and engagement models being adopted across the ecosystem. India's GenZ and millennial shoppers are now harder to reach through traditional media channels and prefer social media networks to make purchase decisions. Hence, brands now want to integrate social and commerce to drive higher awareness, consideration, and sales. Further, Vertical videos are bound to take the centre stage in the coming year, which means long-form or episodic content will create opportunities for influencers to integrate brands into their content with the help of data-driven insights- brands and influencers will churn more personalized content for their followers'

The rise of social commerce in India will also give a fillip to digital-first brands while opening up newer avenues for influencers to monetize from brand collaborations, making it a full-time profession. With this, the industry is all set to create transforming shopping experiences and become more interactive, immersive, and entertaining. Live commerce is one of such innovations where an influencer demonstrates product usability in a live video setting, driving higher visibility, excitement, and loyalty for consumers.

Gautam Madhavan, CEO, Mad Influence:

Short Video and Live Stream will dominate in the influencer marketing industry. Consumers are becoming restless in watching long-format videos - hence they want to consume the on-the-go type of content. Original Content will be one of the key factors driving this. Content Quality and content authenticity is somcthing consumers will be wanting.

CHAPTER TWO

CHATBOTS AND AI

Chatbots are one of the latest trends on social media. It has become increasingly simple for people to reach out to brands through social media.

This makes it very important for brands to respond to their queries on social media as quickly as possible. While it can be a difficult task to get a human to respond instantly, chatbots can come to the rescue in such situations.

What's more?

AI is the future of social media marketing and with it, you can have conversations with your customers. Chatbots powered by AI is being used on Messenger by many brands to promote their products and even resolve customers' issues. A great chatbot you can use for your business is Collect. chat. This chatbot can help you schedule meetings and collect leads on social media with ease.

What's more?

You don't require any technical knowledge to build this chatbot. It can be built using its easy-to-use drag and drop chatbot builder.

Mastercard, for instance, has a chatbot that talks to you about your expenditures and finances.

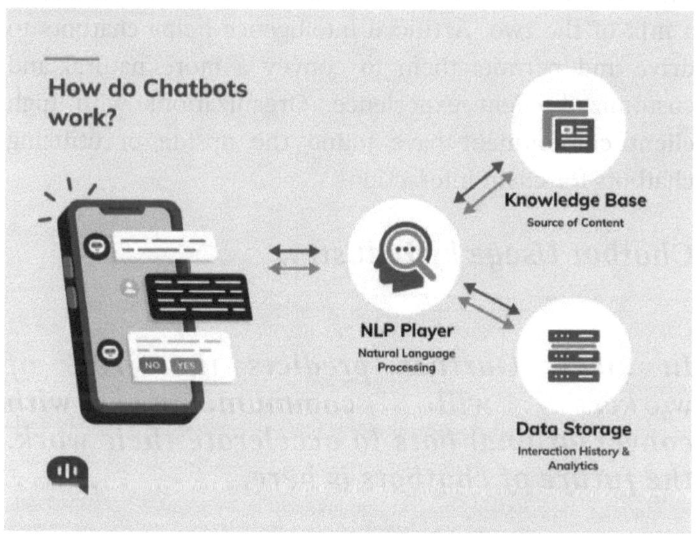

Image via chatbotsjournal

Due to improvements in AI, more brands are switching to this mode of customer service to improve customer satisfaction levels. It can come in handy to answer common questions which may not require any human intervention. At the identical time, the quick responses also result in immediate problem resolution for the customers. With a lot of ongoing development in the field of AI, it can be safely assumed that chatbots are here to stay.

For what reason is Chatbot in India evolving essential for businesses?

A Chatbot is a programming application that can speak with individuals through live chat or other customer support platforms. Their UI is text-based, voice-based, or a mix of the two. Artificial intelligence helps chatbots to drive and permits them to convey a more natural and customized client experience. Organizations with high client commitment have found the upside of utilizing chatbots for client interactions.

Chatbot Usage by Industry:

In 2022, Gartner predicts that 70% of workers will communicate with conversational bots to accelerate their work, the future of chatbots is here.

In 2022, Chatbots will go to different places that they have not gone previously. From client collaborations, intelligent bots will be used casually afterward. In 2022, Gartner predicts that 70% of workers will collaborate with conversational bots to accelerate their work. For example, assuming Martin normally went through a 6-step process to recover explicit records for a task, all he wants to do now is talk or text the chatbot to recover the document. The bot will find and return with relevant records – simple isn't it?

The Future of Chatbots – Top Trends to Look for in 2022-25

Man-made consciousness (AI) is changing chatbots by copying human reasoning and navigation. As per Gartner, by 2022, AI will oversee 70% of all purchaser contacts. However, it isn't just client care, as referenced previously, a huge number of new trends will make their essence felt in more business processes.

Chatbot Service will Deal with Greater Payment Processes.

Chatbots for client support will track options to include payment alternatives. It will be very easy as basic as a client messaging "I need to purchase the latest iPhone" on an online eCommerce portal and the AI chatbot would direct them via the process of selection, until the last step. At the point when a client inputs a request, the bot will give an API request and give a payment link to finish the transaction.

More bots will associate with payment portals like Paypal, online wallets, and other payment portals in 2022. This will permit clients to make payments while never leaving the chatting platform.

By interfacing with the payment infrastructure, organizations can give chatbots enough information to urge discussion-driven upselling to purchasers. The equivalent is used to offer reports on a client's exchange information, payment confirmation, cost records, etc, bringing about a significant level of client retention and confidence.

The Future of Chatbot Service – Voice Bots

Voice Bots are most certainly the following distinct advantage! As indicated by a Forbes article, voice searches will represent the greater part of all inquiries by 2022. Users will prefer messaging services with voice and text-based interfaces. “Alright Google, what’s on my timetable today?” is a common way for users to start their day.

No doubt it revolves around giving users a seamless experience in your organization. Voice bots can assist you with doing that.

With expanding human dependence on these bots, there is a developing reception of voice-recognition ability. Especially in businesses like protection, the travel industry, and instruction. Normal Language Processing (NLP) likewise works with various dialects that engage with pauses of human speech. We are for the most part acquainted with Siri, Alexa, and Google and the amount more human they sound throughout the long term.

While chat (text) is more well known in the developing business sectors. Europe and North America will keep on having ‘voice’ as the biggest contact channel liked by clients.

Virtual assistants that utilize voice capability, a different innovation utilized for chatbots. Voice bots need to acknowledge and discourse the speaker’s intent. Voice bots need to comprehend the speaker’s intent, convert it into text for operating, and afterward, convey a vocal back – all very quickly.

More Humanlike Chatbot

Chatbots are turning out to be more "human-like". Truth be told, a significant number of the informing client assistance stages monitor conversational AI bots. Clients regularly uniform that it's not human on the opposite side. As indicated by figures, organizations will develop emotional intelligence bots to add soft skills to make bots show more "compassion".

To decipher human feelings, chatbots connect with sentiment technology. As a result, a chatbot may now react emotionally to the feelings of customers. "how may I help you?" may change to "Hello, we know that from where you're coming from" utilizing the capacity to understand people at their core.

Chatbots rely upon to turn out to be more mindful of a client's enthusiastic condition in 2022, passing by industry expectations. Accordingly, we expect that organizations will create chatbots that react to customer demands or questions relying upon their feeling as analyzed by the sentiment analysis software.

Intuitive Analytics and Deep Insights with Chatbot Service India

An Accenture report features that 56% of organizations guarantee chatbots are driving interruption in their industry. It's difficult to appropriately conceive client practices and encounters without a profound integration of AI chatbots in business processes. 2022 will be an extraordinary year to deliver chatbot insights and practices since nearly all organization processes are moving to chatbots.

These chatbots monitor the inquiries posed, the reactions given, and the requests sent to specialists. This information might be utilized by organizations to upgrade services in real-time.

In 2022, chatbots will be more prepared to exactly gauge and search keywords, preferences, and satisfaction utilizing chatbots services. Analytics and insights of knowledge, permitting organizations to make further ties and connections with clients.

Multilingual Chatbot India

Let us assume that a person communicates in Italian and is not very convenient or fluent in speaking English. When you are chatting with a chatbot, would you not lean toward the choice to pick a language you are comfortable with to clarify your query and get an answer in a similar language? Chatbots that do this will get moment positive response for organizations that utilize them.

Organizations are understanding the significance of multi-lingual chatbots to further develop their localization efforts and widen their reach. Regardless you are in any part of the world, you are probably going to need clients from everywhere on this globe. NLP chatbots (normal language processing) prepare to naturally distinguish the client's language or even utilize the IP locations to recognize the geographic areas.

At present upon observing a fast ascent in organizations embracing multilingual AI chatbot abilities. Each social networking platform will shortly commit to this board.

Advantageous Virtual Assistance – Chatbot Service India

One of the most common and favorable advantages is that chatbot combines different applications and tasks. This gives chatbot an edge over using numerous separate applications while assisting the automation of different customer services.

What does the future for business chatbot service India resemble?

Chatbots that are carelessly positioned will disappear in a fast-developing conversational AI industry. Just those that have been cautiously planned and deployed across all channels will be able to continuously live. A huge number of clients will favor voice-enabled conversational AI to associate with organizations across every platform. Moreover, unique chatbot applications will never be confined. Organizations may build up a chatbot intranet where they could trade and exchange information without any problem. In the meantime, AI-based chatbot service will keep on expanding client commitment and further develop customer service.

CHAPTER THREE

EMPLOYEE ADVOCACY

With the rise of influencer marketing, there has been a rise in the number of fake influencers too. These people fake partnerships with brands to promote themselves and become real influencers.

Brands need to put a lot of resources and time into analyzing influencers and their social media presence to figure out their authenticity. In a time when it can become difficult to trust influencers, employee advocacy will rise.

Your employees can become influencers for your brand among their circles on social media. You can encourage your employees to talk about your brand on social media to promote it among their groups.

One way of doing this can be by giving some share-worthy social media content to them. Alternatively, you can give them some incentive to promote your brand on social media as well.

So, how can you get your employees to post about your brand on social media?

You can employ tools like DrumUp. This platform lets you release company updates to employees and makes it easy for them to share them on social media. Employees can schedule the social media posts with a single click and help spread the word about your brand online.

What's more?

This platform also helps you incorporate an industry news stream so that you can keep your employees updated with the latest news in the industry.

Employees can be viewed as trusted sources of information for a brand. Getting them to promote your brand can help you gain traction on social media. This trend may dictate the future of social media marketing and influencer marketing.

How to build employee advocacy processes

We've put together a six-step process to help you create a successful employee advocacy platform that empowers your team and helps to increase brand awareness and reach.

1. Ensure you have a positive work environment

If you aren't facilitating a positive and engaged company culture, your employees won't be interested in promoting your business for you. Take the necessary steps to make sure your employees are proud to represent your company. A few ideas include:

- **Create an environment that allows employees to do their best work.** This may be offering a remote work option or a four-day workweek, the technology needed to get their jobs done, comfortable and adjustable desk/chair options, or building an asynchronous culture that prioritizes deep work over real-time replies.
- **Provide positive feedback and reinforcements.** Regularly give your employees positive feedback. If they only hear negative criticisms, they're not going to feel good about the work they're doing for you and won't buy into advocacy.
- **Celebrate special occasions.** Celebrate your employees and their monumental moments. Be it a work anniversary, buying a home, having a baby, getting married, a birthday, a successful side hustle, or something else.
- **Hold regular check-ins.** Empower employees to come to you to talk about ideas or concerns. Holding a formal check-in every so often, whether quarterly or annually, is a great way to do so. Even an informal check-in via email or Slack can move mountains.
- **Invest in your employees.** Show employees that you genuinely care about their success. Pay them what they're worth. Reward them with gifts. Invest in new learning opportunities like conferences and courses.

Bottom line: show your employees that you know their worth and that you appreciate them every step of the way. Build a positive culture, and you're sure to have employees excited to represent your brand online.

2. Set goals and objectives

The next step is to set specific goals and objectives for your advocacy policy. Leveraging employees as brand advocates can be a great way to improve company culture, but a formal employee advocacy program should plan to meet specific metrics and KPIs.

For example:

- Increase social media followers (across all social media channels) by X# in an X time frame
- Increase in organic reach by X% over an X time frame
- Generate more website traffic from social networks over X period
- Build higher social media engagement over X period
- Catalyze word of mouth marketing and referrals (measure by X new referrals in an X time frame, as well as the quality of referrals)

Be sure to create SMART goals (Specific, Measurable, Achievable, Realistic, and anchored within a Time Frame). Give each one a specific numeric goal that you hope to achieve. This is the most effective way to know if you're hitting your KPIs or if you need to adjust your program.

3. Pinpoint leaders and participants

Decide who's going to lead the charge, as well as who should participate as the first group of employee advocates. having set leadership to keep your team excited about this program is key. You don't want to launch, watch a group of employees shares content consistently for a month or two, then have the enthusiasm die down before reaping any benefits.

The program needs to be consistently nurtured to maximize employee engagement—a set of team leaders can zero in on achieving goals without losing focus.

As for your pilot group of advocates, consider those who are already active on social media. They'll be most likely to adapt to the new marketing strategy quickly, and likely already have a decent following. Testing it out with your company's marketers is another great place to start.

Make sure to explain the benefits of employee advocacy to get this test group jazzed about the project. Benefits include:

- **Building a strong personal brand.** Having an active social media presence can lead to a greater following and a larger personal and professional network.
- **Becoming a thought leader in your industry.** Sharing content and starting conversations around your brand or industry will generate attention and help your employees to position themselves as thought leaders.
- **Incentives and gamification rewards.** To keep the advocacy program exciting, consider offering incentives like gift cards or a bonus. Gamifying the process by keeping a leaderboard of employees garnering the most engagement is another way to make advocacy more fun.

The end goal is to empower interested employees to become true advocates for your brand. Their passion should be self-driven and rely on passion more than incentive-driven rewards.

It should not feel like a forced job, or else it will come across as a forced post. It should look and feel like a natural extension of their social presence.

Starting with a small group is a great way to test the waters and see if this is a tactic that will work well for your team.

4. Create social media guidelines for employees

Once you've identified the employees who will lead and test your new advocacy solution, put together social media guidelines and brand messages for them to adhere to. this is something Starbucks has done for their employee advocates or "partners" (as they like to call them). the two-page document has a list of do's and don'ts, as well as contact information if the advocate has made a mistake and needs to work with the social media team directly for crisis management.

Your social media guidelines can be as long or as short as you want them. It's a good idea to work with your human resources team to make sure you cover all your bases before sending employees off to publicly curate company content.

This document should include information like:

- Examples of the types of posts they could create
- The tone of voice guidelines
- Hashtags to use
- Reminders that they're an advocate, not a company spokesperson

- Details about your brand's target audience
- Do's and don'ts for best representing your brand
- Who to contact if something goes wrong (and how to reach them)

5. Put together a library of assets and resources

Compile a library of assets that members can choose from to promote, as well as resources on how to get the most out of this strategy.

You want to set your employees up for success. An internal resource like this sets the tone, provides valuable information, and offers support.

Consider compiling:

- Photos and graphics to use as post visuals
- Links to the content you'd like to see promoted (although the most natural posts are from people who are also involved in creating said content)
- Sample captions or talking points to jumpstart their posts
- Internal communication or online resources explaining more about how to get the most out of employee advocacy
- Recent company news and milestones

6. Keep your employee advocacy program going

The last step is to put a system in place to keep your employees sharing regular updates about your brand. have your social media marketing team regularly update your asset library with new content and visuals. Consider creating a channel or group in your team's online communication tool to share exciting company updates and talking points. talking about a brand on social media shouldn't be reserved only for the C-suite. By empowering employees of all levels to be a part of the company and share related content, you're cultivating a strong company culture and helping increase employee retention along the way

CHAPTER FOUR

Driving Sales Through Social Media

While social media has long been used to generate engagement and sales, the latter is becoming a solid trend. Brands are provided with the necessary tools to promote their products on social media to get sales. With advanced tracking tools such as the Facebook Pixel, it is possible to chart out the buyer journey as well. However, for this, you need to keep publishing good social media content regularly.

So, how can you achieve this?

To simplify publishing on social media, you can leverage platforms. It allows you to create and publish your campaigns directly on social media. You can also schedule your posts well in advance so that you can publish them exactly when you want them to be posted. Using the tool, you can also monitor your social mentions and engage with your audience. This can help you increase your sales.According to Kleiner Perkins, about 55% of people who found a product on social media purchased it later. Among social media channels, Facebook is the leading platform for product discovery. Instagram and Pinterest are closely catching up in this trend as well.This means that you can promote your products on these social media platforms to generate consistent sales. It is not necessary to rely on sales pitches anymore.With social media, you can catch the attention of your target consumers and get them to purchase from you. Paid promotions on social media for your products should definitely be a part of your social media marketing strategy.

Social is now a fixture in the customer journey and has a direct impact on purchasing decisions. Starting at the top of the funnel, **consumers increasingly use social** to discover new brands, products and services, which is good news for your awareness goals and prospective sales. The consumers in discovery mode that go on to hit the follow button really mean business.

According to the latest **Sprout Social Index™**, 90% of consumers will purchase from a brand they follow on social media. Your followers are also more likely to choose your brand over a competitor, visit your physical store and other actions that push sales in a positive direction.

Not only are consumer shopping preferences shifting to social, social platform developers are actively bringing sales and social marketing closer together with the steady emergence of new or improved **social commerce** solutions.

As your business looks to social media to increase online sales and turn a profit, apply these five simple tactics to your strategy.

1. Start selling directly on social media platforms

Social commerce is booming, thanks in part to the pandemic accelerating digital transformation. As physical spaces shut down, digital storefronts went up. In 2020, Facebook, Instagram, and Pinterest launched revamped social commerce tools, and Twitter, YouTube and TikTok announced that they too were exploring social commerce for their platforms.

As social platforms increase their investments in commerce solutions, businesses are following suit—86% of executives say **social commerce is a growing part of their marketing-driven revenue plan.** Social commerce encapsulates the entire customer journey, allowing consumers to move from discovery to purchase in a single channel. And with a frictionless shopping experience and streamlined checkout process, consumers are more likely to make purchases in the moment.

Connecting your product catalogs to a social commerce solution also gives brands a chance to curate collections that align with larger campaigns. **Sprout's dedicated integrations with Shopify and Facebook Shops** make it easy to accelerate your entry to social commerce. Once users upload their product catalogs into Sprout, they can add product links to social content or include them in responses to consumers who have reached out directly.

2. Find your highest converting social content—and make more of it

Data and social best practices suggest that **visual content helps marketers hit social goals** more than text-based posts, but maybe your audience is different. The only way to know is to track your own social success, dig into the data and make more of what works.

For the sake of understanding how social media can increase sales, focus your analysis on owned content that includes information about your products or services, promotions, and links to your website. Ideally those links will include **UTM parameters** so you can effectively track the behavior and path of people who have clicked the link via Google Analytics.

What data matters most? Here's a quick breakdown of the KPIs you should be on the lookout for.

- **Organic**: Engagement rate, click-through-rate, social traffic referrals, website page actions (e.g., form submissions, purchases)
- **Paid**: Conversion rate, return on ad spend (RoAS), cost per conversion

Marketers who are diligent about tagging outbound content have the ability to conduct more granular analysis. For example, **fashion retailer River Island** has over 160 active tags they apply to content to track more qualitative insights like consumers' preferences for UGC content versus official brand photography.

Using Sprout's Tag Performance Report, they can analyze and compare performance, which helps them decide how to allocate budgets for different creative assets and ad campaigns.

Once you identify your audience's preferred content formats, you can look for ways to transform them into **shoppable posts**. Thanks to emerging functionality across social platforms, everything from video to UGC can turn into a conversion opportunity.

3. Use conversational commerce to nurture buyers on social

One of the obvious benefits of social media is that it gives both consumers and businesses a convenient, accessible way to communicate with one another—**78% of consumers agree that social is the fastest and most direct way to connect with a brand.**

Conversational commerce combines messaging and shopping, enabling consumers to use chat or voice assistance to make purchases from a brand. **Chris Messina**, who coined the term, says it's all about "delivering convenience, personalization and decision support while people are on the go, with only partial attention to spare."

If you've ever received a promotional code or discount in your direct messages, booked a haircut appointment through Facebook Messenger, or asked a product question in WhatsApp, that's conversational commerce at work. Across platforms, messaging allows digital marketers to deepen customer relationships by offering more personalized recommendations like a digital personal shopper.

It's important to note that conversational commerce isn't solely about net-new sales. Offering strong customer service is an equally important benefit, and pays its own dividends given that it's the top-quality consumers associate with best-in-class brands on social.

No matter where a customer falls in the sales funnel, social marketers need to have a strategy in place to manage inbound messages and provide efficient, effective support. **MeUndies**, an underwear and loungewear brand, has a robust social commerce strategy—so it's no surprise that their customers most frequently seek support on social. Using Sprout Social's Smart Inbox, MeUndies can tag, analyze and respond to customer inquiries via Messenger with ease. With Message tags let the customer experience team evaluate the types of inquiries they receive most frequently, and share that information with sales teams and leadership.

Their top-tier social customer service strategy drives sales and incredible customer loyalty— the proof is on social.

4. Use social listening to find which topics resonate with your audience

It pays to know your audience. When brands demonstrate that they understand their customers" wants and needs, **43% of consumers will buy from that brand over their competitor**.

Social listening lets businesses tap into public conversations that expand their understanding of their customers, industry, and competitors. It can give insight into the **trends your audiences are engaging with**, reveal sentiment around specific brand campaigns, and opportunities to differentiate your brand from the competition. Social listening holds the **answers to your business' burning questions** and with knowledge comes power.

Combine your findings from social listening with your insights from content analytics and customer service channels to develop data-backed marketing messaging that converts.

Social listening can also surface leads and sales opportunities for your brand, you just have to be ready to jump in. Black Girl Sunscreen, for example, wasn't mentioned in the original Tweet below. But with social listening, their team flagged the relevant prompt and responded accordingly.

Harnessing the power of social listening is much simpler if you have tools like Sprout Social that do the heavy lifting for you. **Empower your sales team to master social listening with this step-by-step guide.**

5. Check that you're posting on social at the right time (for your audience)

Posting content at the right time often means more impressions, engagement, and conversions. Data will tell you, for example, that **the worst time to post on Facebook is Saturday**. But your audience is unique. Analyze your own social platforms and find what times work best for you, then build a publishing schedule from there.

- **Facebook**: Optimal send content had 62% more impressions, had 135% more engagement
- **Twitter**: 59% more impressions, 97% more engagement
- **Instagram**: 44% more impressions, 65% more engagement

Publishing at the right time creates more exposure for your brand and, ultimately, more chances to entice a sale.

CHAPTER FIVE

THE IMPORTANCE OF ENGAGEMENT

The engagement has always mattered on social media. However, with the change in Facebook's algorithm that emphasizes meaningful interactions, it has become even more important. This means that content that starts genuine conversations has become more favored.

So, what should you do?

To improve your organic reach, your content needs to be highly engaging. That means it should be interesting and appealing to your target audience too. It's not enough to just ask people to like, share, and comment on your posts on social media.

You need to change your approach and move away from engagement baiting techniques. Genuine content is the key to success in the future of social media marketing.

Why engagement rates are important on social media?

They offer social proof of your business social media engagement extends beyond the number of Instagram followers you have or the number of likes you've accumulated on your business's Facebook page. It does, of course, have a bearing on how your business is perceived by a prospective customer but how you're engaging with your fans is what's going to force people to pay attention.

If followers are commenting on your posts saying how much they love your content, products, or services, new visitors are naturally inclined to think that if other people enjoy working with you, they will too. Social media

Engagement is so powerful it can offer the same kind of social proof as a testimonial from a satisfied customer. In turn, this makes people more likely to purchase your product or service. Increased engagement boosts brand awareness Social media has the power to bring people closer together irrespective of borders and oceans in between. For businesses, this means the world's oyster when it comes to extending their reach.

Every time an individual interacts with you on social media, overall awareness of your brand increases. Someone simply following or liking your page won't always show up on anyone else's newsfeed, however. If they're liking, commenting on, or sharing your content, this is what's going to get you seen by new audiences. Blossom by First Media received a huge amount of publicity back in 2017 when one of its Facebook videos went viral. It was a short and simple video providing tips on getting clever with your clutter and people loved it so much it was viewed over 400 million times, received 12 million shares, over three million likes, and nearly a quarter of a million comments.

Engagement plays a significant role in social media algorithms each social media platform has a unique set of technical elements and user analytics. This data is analyzed and used to create an algorithm that delivers content to its users. Put into layman's terms, engagement affects the visibility of your content.

The more people interact with your posts, the more likely your content is to show up in their newsfeed. The reason for this is that if someone never likes your content, sites like Facebook assume they're not interested in it. If you're regularly liking, commenting, or sharing someone's posts, however, Facebook knows you're interested in what they have to say.

Dealing with social media algorithms can be frustrating (especially because they like to change them every so often). They can also be beneficial to small businesses, however. You may feel it's impossible to compete with the larger brands but with everyone being forced to focus on creating high-value content that provokes a reaction, it means that businesses of all sizes can reach out to their followers. Knowing what each platform prioritizes can help you beat the algorithms and boost engagement.

Facebook

When deciding what content to show its users, Facebook now puts posts "that spark conversations and meaningful interactions" at the top of people's news feed. Some great ways to do this include:

1. Create content that's going to evoke stronger reactions than a simple like. Facebook introduced reactions in 2016 so users can now show love, anger, sadness, amazement, or even laugh at the content they're seeing. Few people realize the
2. importance of the reaction feature but it
3. does have a higher weightage than likes when it comes to prioritizing content.
4. Shares have a huge influence on the number of people who see your posts on Facebook. The site prioritizes content that comes from friends and family as opposed to fan pages.
5. Comments are another great way to ensure you're appearing in the news feeds of your followers and even the people they're connected with. Popular or topical news articles are great at prompting discussion as are interactive posts. If you run a bakery, for example, you could ask your followers what their favorite type of cake is.

6. If you're brave enough to go live on

7. Facebook, it's worth noting that it gets six times more interactions than normal videos and is, therefore, a great way to boost engagement.
8. Remind your followers to choose to see your content first through the 'see first' option which can be found on your page's 'following' drop-down menu.

Instagram

What better way to find out how Instagram prioritizes content than to hear it straight from the social media giant themselves? As with all these platforms, there's always confusion about how their algorithms work so Instagram addressed the issue directly.

If you want to ensure that more people see your content on Instagram, this is the way to do it:

1. Use good quality photos. This is a given considering it's a photo-sharing platform so make sure your imagery is striking and uses bold colors. If it would make you stop in your tracks (or stop scrolling), chances are it will have the same impact on your followers. If you can't afford a professional photographer, there are plenty of apps that can help you create better imagery on a budget.
2. Post stories. Instagram says that stories don't have any influence on their algorithm but considering it's the most popular content on the site, it can still help you gain and retain followers. It also gives people a reason to keep checking back with your page.
3. Go live. Like with the stories, going live doesn't affect Instagram's algorithm. Followers can choose to receive notifications when you go live however and you'll also go to the top of your followers' stories feeds which can dramatically help improve engagement.
4. We know with certainty that Instagram prioritizes engagement so it's important to write compelling captions. Encourage interactions by asking questions or encouraging followers to tag other people in your posts.
5. The more eyes on your posts, the better.
6. Hashtags are very important on Instagram. Without them, your content is limited to the people following

you. By using hashtags, however, you're opening yourself up to a whole new audience.

Twitter

Twitter users can switch between an algorithm feed and a real-time feed. There are some ways your small business could appear on someone's timeline:

Top tweets: an algorithm-powered feed organized by ranking signals. In addition to ranked content from followers, this feed will sometimes feature suggestions about who to follow as well as content from accounts you don't follow. Latest tweets: a reverse-chronological feed of tweets from followers (the most recent tweets appear first).In case you missed it: a short algorithm-powered module of top tweets. The more time a user spends in the app, the less likely they are to see this. Happening now: this section may occasionally appear at the top of user timelines, featuring events or topics of interest. Trends for you: an algorithm-driven section that highlights popular trends and hashtags for users.

While Twitter's CEO has always been insistent about maintaining a real-time platform, some factors affect the site's ranking signals.

How recently the tweet was published

How many retweets, clicks, favorites, or impressions a post has received

The type of media included in the tweet (image, video, GIF, and even polls)

How many followers does an account have

The main thing any small business owner wants to know is how can they use Twitter's algorithms to boost their engagement:

Maintain an active presence – the more positive engagements you have with your followers, the better. The best way to do this is to post regularly. Consistent engagement can also earn you credit with Twitter's algorithm.

Hashtags can drive brand awareness and engagement which can translate into algorithm recognition. It may also land your hashtags in the 'trends for you' section.

Use rich media. Tweets with videos can bring as much as 10x more engagement and GIFs get 55% more engagement.

You must reply to anyone who tweets you or replies to your post from a customer service perspective. Because

Twitter's ranking signals look at account engagement, however, it can also help you beat the algorithm.

Tips on boosting engagement rates

1. I've shared some great tips on boosting engagement rates for each platform above. Several techniques should be standard practice across all your social media channels. This will ensure you're appearing on people's timelines and engaging with your audience in the right way.
2. Respond to every single comment or post people leave on your page.
3. Offer an incentive in return for social sharing. For example, a restaurant can

4. offer customers 10% off their bill if they take a picture of their meal and post it on Instagram. Other companies can offer a
5. discount if customers check in to their
6. Facebook business page or run a competition where followers can win a prize for liking or sharing their post.
7. The best way to build engagement with your followers on any platform is to create content they want to engage with. This could be sharing articles that spark conversation, posting helpful tips, imparting your expertise, or offering discounts.
8. Improving your engagement rates on social media means so much more than just receiving likes or new followers. It's a measurement of how many people are paying attention to and interacting with your brand daily. By focusing on building your social media engagement, your business will benefit from a better marketing reach, greater brand awareness, and an improved ROI.

CHAPTER SIX

THE RISE OF GROUPS

Groups on Facebook have new features such as live video content, story updates, and participation as a business page. With the changes in the algorithm of Facebook, Groups have become the go-to place to connect with your audience in the current social media landscape.

Through Groups, you can not only get feedback about your products but even generate additional engagement.

What's more?

A similar effect has been noticed on Instagram where influencers have started making their profiles private. This is done to avoid the effects of the Instagram algorithm.

An influencer, Karan, turned all of his memes accounts private and found that the growth rate was far better than when he kept them open.

CHAPTER SEVEN

TRANSPARENCY

2018 was a year filled with privacy issues on major social media platforms such as Facebook. GDPR also came into effect to protect the data that websites took from customers.

According to research, only 55% of customers felt that brands were transparent to some extent on social media. On the other hand, only 15% of them felt that they were very transparent.

This powerful statistic shows that there's a lot that brands need to do to grow their transparency on social media. And millennials expect brands to be the most transparent on social media. This means that you need to up the ante by admitting your mistakes or at least giving honest responses to them.

What's more, you ask?

The same survey also found the top desire of consumers is for transparency from brands. That includes business practices, the company's values, and product changes. This means that you should share changes to your products and give a behind-the-scenes look of your company too. You can do so with image posts, video content, and live Q&A sessions.

The greater your transparency on social media, the more consumers trust you. And trust can translate into greater sales. That said, transparency is the way ahead in the future of social media marketing.

CHAPTER EIGHT

STORIES

Stories started out on Snapchat. However, Facebook, Instagram, and WhatsApp quickly adopted this feature too. These primarily vertical Stories usually last 24 hours and give people tremendous opportunities to create different types of content.

About 500 million people watch Instagram Stories every single day. Similarly, Facebook stories can be seen on Messenger and Facebook on the desktop too.

They are highly engaging and due to their interactive nature, they have caught the attention of millennials. As many as 60% of them consume Stories on Instagram, 53% on Snapchat, and 48% on Facebook.

Due to this level of engagement, they have become a popular marketing tool for brands. Additionally, they are easy to create and don't require a lot of post-processing.

The main reason for their success though is that they aren't too long to watch. This makes it very convenient for people to watch them on the go.

What's more?

Recently, even LinkedIn joined the Stories bandwagon. This goes to show their effectiveness. It is thus safe to say that Stories are a powerful trend in the future of social media marketing.

CHAPTER NINE

LIVE VIDEOS

Live video content is another popular trend on social media. Live videos were launched first on YouTube in 2008 and then on Facebook in 2016. Even Instagram added this feature later on.

What's more, you ask?

A study conducted by Brandlive noted that about 95% of marketers were planning to add live videos to their social media marketing strategies. There are a lot of things you can do through live videos such as launching new products.

You can even demonstrate your products and create how-to live videos. This can help your audience get acquainted with the product better too.

for example, used Facebook Live to create a how-to video for their products. A live video gives your audience the opportunity to interact with you in real-time and clear their doubts.

This can help generate additional engagement and make the interaction exciting for them too.

You can even give your brand a more human touch by creating Q&A live video sessions. These add a human element and allow the consumers to get their doubts solved during the video itself by talking to you.

image from google search

CHAPTER TEN

IMPORTANCE OF MESSAGING

Messaging apps have started giving serious competition to traditional social media platforms. People want to move beyond commenting on posts and want to interact with their close circles personally.

This makes messaging very favorable for them. WhatsApp, Messenger, and WeChat have garnered above 1 billion active monthly users.

Brands need to understand how people use messaging apps to get their desired reach and engagement.

image from Google

Many brands have started sending out messages to customers on WhatsApp to build connections on a personal level.

This includes Absolut Vodka, which launched a campaign for an exclusive party. To enter the party, people had to message an imaginary bouncer and convince him to let them in. This led to over 1,000 unique images, videos, and audios aimed at convincing the bouncer

CHAPTER ELEVEN

AUGMENTED REALITY

We may not realize it but we're already using AR when we use the filters on Instagram, Facebook, or Snapchat. It's possible to give your face different looks through it and click photos and videos. Facebook Messenger has even made it possible to use AR during video calls.

While it hasn't been used to market products yet, there may soon come a time when we may have branded AR. For instance, you may be able to try on branded glasses and purchase them right away.

Instagram has already rolled out such features and we may soon see more brands adopting it on the platform.

image from Google search

AR is not only fun to try and experiment with but is even actionable. This makes it a very useful tool for marketing. Facebook has already announced the introduction of such AR ads to make shopping on Facebook even more appealing. This might as well become a trend in the future of social media marketing.

What Is Artificial Intelligence For Social Media

AI in social media holds the potential to transform how brands market across networks like Facebook, Instagram, Twitter, and LinkedIn.

It can automate many tedious tasks related to social media management.

And it can even do social media monitoring at scale.

That might be why the "AI in social media" market is projected to grow from $633 million in 2018 to more than $2.1 billion by 2023, according to estimates

But what actually is artificial intelligence?

How can AI in social media actually impact your marketing and analytics?

And, most importantly, how do you actually get started using artificial intelligence for social media?

This article is here to help.

At Marketing Artificial Intelligence Institute, we've spent years helping marketers understand and apply artificial intelligence, so they can increase revenue and reduce costs at their companies.

And social media marketing is one of the main areas where marketers can both skyrocket performance and efficiencies by using artificial intelligence, getting more value and engagement out of every online conversation that happens on social media channels.

In this post, we'll demystify artificial intelligence, then show you how exactly it can be used in your social media marketing.

What is artificial intelligence?

Ask 10 different experts what artificial intelligence is, and you'll get 10 different answers. But one definition we like comes from Demis Hassabis, CEO of DeepMind, an AI startup acquired by Google.

Hassabis calls artificial intelligence the "science of making machines smart."

Basically, we can teach machines to be like humans. We can give them the ability to see, hear, speak, move, and write.

You use AI every day, no matter where you work or what you do.

Your smartphone has dozens of native capabilities powered by AI, such as voice assistants and real-time navigation.

Your favorite services, like Amazon and Netflix, use AI to offer product recommendations.

And email clients like Gmail even use AI to automatically write parts of emails for you.

Many of AI's most impressive capabilities are powered by machine learning, a subset of AI that enables machine systems to make accurate predictions based on large sets of data.

The smartest AI tools than actually improve the accuracy of their predictions over time using machine learning and deep learning, an advanced type of machine learning.

It's this last part that makes AI and machine learning different from traditional software or technology platforms.

Your typical non-AI software is coded by humans, then follows the instructions humans have given it. These systems only get better when humans manually make them better.

AI tools, on the other hand, can improve on their own, based on both their own historical performance and new data given to the system-unlocking potentially unlimited performance gains.

That means every piece of marketing software you use today, from ad buying to analytics to automation to content strategy to social, can be made more intelligent using AI and machine learning.

These tools can then be trained to leverage indiv idual behaviors, preferences, beliefs, and interests to personalize experiences.

They can understand where you've been, where you're going, what you've written in emails, what you've asked your voice assistants, what groups you belong to, what stores you shop at, and more.

All of this data becomes fuel for artificially intelligent systems.

Those systems use the information to make increasingly relevant and accurate predictions about everything from what product you want to buy next to which ad campaign to run to which content topics to cover on your blog.And it gives AI tools some amazing capabilities that traditional technology just doesn't have.AI can read and write using natural language generation and natural language processing.It can detect and mimic tone of voice using sentiment analysis.It can detect images, video, and faces using image recognition and computer vision capabilities.AI can even predict performance and recommend actions.These capabilities can be used to give your social media marketing superpowers.

How is AI used in social media?

AI is a key component of the popular social networks you use every single day.

Facebook uses advanced machine learning to do everything from serve you content to recognize your face in photos to target users with advertising. Instagram (owned by Facebook) uses AI to identify visuals.LinkedIn uses AI to offer job recommendations, suggest people you might like to connect with and serve you specific posts in your feed. Snapchat leverages the power of computer vision, and AI technology, to track your features and overlay filters that move with your face in real-time. These are just a few examples of how AI works behind the scenes to power features of the world's most popular social networks. And, across all social media platforms and each social media post, an AI algorithm or machine learning system is regulating how the content you create and the ads you buy are placed in front of users-often in ways that aren't entirely transparent to marketers.

This is all to say that AI is a fundamental part of how today's social networks function.But, AI often operates behind the scenes of popular platforms, and entirely at the discretion of the company that owns the platform.

However, that doesn't mean marketers can't leverage AI for their social media strategy.

In fact, there are many commercially available artificial intelligence social media monitoring and marketing tools across a number of use cases.

Here are a few of the top ways social media marketers can start using AI, machine learning, and intelligent automation technologies. Social creation and management marketers spend a ton of time creating content for social media distribution, then managing distribution and engagement across channels.

A traditional social media management tool helps with this, by streamlining social media scheduling and monitoring. But AI tools take it further.

Tools exist to auto-generate social media content across channels, going so far as to automatically include hashtags and shortened links. Tools also exist to auto-schedule these shares in bulk.

Overall, an AI tool is able-today-to handle certain types of social media creation and management in minutes. Social media intelligence and social media listening AI-powered social monitoring tool or social listening tool can deliver insights from your brand's social media profiles and audience. This often involves using the power of AI to analyze social data at scale, understand what's being said in them, then extract insights based on that information. That data, properly applied, allows AI social media monitoring tools to:

Help you track your global brand mentions
Find emerging consumer trends
Find new audiences to target
Keep tabs on brand reputation
Monitor every social mention
Identify promising new avenues for social media promotion.

These actionable insights are delivered in near real-time, giving brands a leg up against the competition.

Social media advertising

Almost any social media platform gives marketers an unprecedented ability to run paid ads to platform users based on highly granular demographic and behavioral targeting. But marketers still need to write or create ad creative...or do they? Artificial intelligence tools exist today that will actually write Facebook and Instagram ads for you. The ads are optimized for clicks and conversions, thanks to AI's ability to predict at scale which language will improve results. Find the right influencer finding the right influencer can put a brand on the map. But how do you do so efficiently? AI can lend a hand. AI-powered influencer research platforms analyze a variety of social media analytics to understand which accounts can provide the most engagement, reach, and influence for a specific industry.

Metaverse

What Is the Metaverse?

The metaverse is a concept of a persistent, online, 3D universe that combines multiple different virtual spaces. You can think of it as a future iteration of the internet. The metaverse will allow users to work, meet, game, and socialize together in these 3D spaces.

The metaverse isn't fully in existence, but some platforms contain metaverse-like elements. Video games currently provide the closest metaverse experience on offer. Developers have pushed the boundaries of what a game is through hosting in-game events and creating virtual economies.

Although not required, cryptocurrencies can be a great fit for a metaverse. They allow for creating a digital economy with different types of utility tokens and virtual collectibles (NFTs). The metaverse would also benefit from the use of crypto wallets, such as Trust Wallet and MetaMask. Also, blockchain technology can provide transparent and reliable governance systems.

Blockchain, metaverse-like applications already exist and provide people with liveable incomes. Axie Infinity is one play-to-earn game that many users play to support their income. SecondLife and Decentraland are other examples of successfully mixing the blockchain world and virtual reality apps.

When we look to the future, big tech giants are trying to lead the way. However, the decentralized aspects of the blockchain industry is letting smaller players participate in the metaverse's development as well.

Introduction

The connections between the financial, virtual, and physical worlds have become increasingly linked. The devices we use to manage our lives give us access to almost anything we want at the touch of a button. The crypto ecosystem hasn't escaped this either. NFTs, blockchain games, and crypto payments aren't just limited to crypto geeks anymore. They're now all easily available as part of a developing metaverse.

What's the definition of a metaverse?

The metaverse is a concept of an online, 3D, virtual space connecting users in all aspects of their lives. It would connect multiple platforms, similar to the internet containing different websites accessible through a single browser.

The concept was developed in the science-fiction novel Snow Crash by Neal Stephenson. However, while the idea of a metaverse was once fiction, it now looks like it could be a reality in the future.

The metaverse will be driven by augmented reality, with each user controlling a character or avatar. For example, you might take a mixed reality meeting with an Oculus VR headset in your virtual office, finish work and relax in a blockchain-based game, and then manage your crypto portfolio and finances all inside the metaverse.

You can already see some aspects of the metaverse in existing virtual video game worlds. Games like Second Life and Fortnite or work socialization tools like Gather.town bring together multiple elements of our lives into online worlds. While these applications are not the metaverse, they are somewhat similar. The metaverse still doesn't exist yet.

Besides supporting gaming or social media, the metaverse will combine economies, digital identity, decentralized governance, and other applications. Even today, user creation and ownership of valuable items and currencies help develop a single, united metaverse. All these features provide blockchain the potential to power this future technology.

Why are video games linked to the metaverse?

Because of the emphasis on 3D virtual reality, video games offer the closest metaverse experience currently. This point isn't just because they are 3D, though. Video games now offer services and features that cross over into other aspects of our lives. The video game Roblox even hosts virtual events like concerts and meetups. Players don't just play the game anymore; they also use it for other activities and parts of their lives in "cyberspace". For example, in the multiplayer game Fortnite, 12.3 million players took part in Travis Scott's virtual in-game music tour.

How does crypto fit into the metaverse?

Gaming provides the 3D aspect of the metaverse but doesn't cover everything needed in a virtual world that can cover all aspects of life. Crypto can offer the other key parts required, such as digital proof of ownership, transfer of value, governance, and accessibility. But what do these mean exactly?

If in the future, we work, socialize, and even purchase virtual items in the metaverse, we need a secure way of showing ownership. We also need to feel safe transferring these items and money around the metaverse. Finally, we will also want to play a role in the decision-making taking place in the metaverse if it will be such a large part of our lives.

Some video games contain some basic solutions already, but many developers use crypto and blockchain instead as a better option. Blockchain provides a decentralized and transparent way of dealing with the topics, while video-game development is more centralized.

Blockchain developers also take influence from the video game world too. Gamification is common in Decentralized Finance (Defi) and GameFi. It seems there will be enough similarities in the future that the two worlds may become even more integrated. The key aspects of blockchain suited to the metaverse are:

1. Digital proof of ownership: By owning a wallet with access to your private keys, you can instantly prove ownership of activity or an asset on the blockchain. For example, you could show an exact transcript of your transactions on the blockchain while at work to show accountability. A wallet is one of the most secure and robust methods for establishing a digital identity and proof of ownership.

2. Digital collectibility: Just as we can establish who owns something, we can also show that an item is original and unique. For a metaverse looking to incorporate more real-life activities, this is important. Through NFTs, we can create objects that are 100% unique and can never be copied exactly or forged. A blockchain can also represent

ownership of physical items.

3. Transfer of value: A metaverse will need a way to transfer value securely that users trust. In-game currencies in multiplayer games are less secure than crypto on a blockchain. If users spend large amounts of time in the metaverse and even earn money there, they will need a reliable currency.

4. Governance: The ability to control the rules of your interaction with the metaverse should also be important for users. In real life, we can have voting rights in companies and elect leaders and governments. The metaverse will also need ways to implement fair governance, and blockchain is already a proven way of doing this.

5. Accessibility: Creating a wallet is open to anyone around the world on public blockchains. Unlike a bank account, you don't need to pay any money or provide any details. This makes it one of the most accessible ways to manage finances and online, digital identity.

6. Interoperability: Blockchain technology is continuously improving compatibility between different platforms. Projects like Polkadot (DOT) and Avalanche (AVAX) allow for creating custom blockchains that can interact with each other. A single metaverse will need to connect multiple projects, and blockchain technology already has solutions for this.

What's the future of the metaverse?

Facebook is one of the loudest voices for the creation of a unified metaverse. This is particularly interesting for a crypto-powered metaverse due to Facebook's Diem stablecoin project. Mark Zuckerberg has explicitly mentioned his plans to use a metaverse project to support remote work and improve financial opportunities for people in developing countries. Facebook's ownership of social media, communication, and crypto platforms give it a good start combining all these worlds into one. Other large tech companies are also targeting the creation of a metaverse, including Microsoft, Apple, and Google.

When it comes to a crypto-powered metaverse, further integration between NFT marketplaces and 3D virtual universes seems like the next step. NFT holders can already sell their goods from multiple sources on marketplaces like OpenSea and BakerySwap, but there isn't yet a popular 3D platform for this. At a bigger scale, blockchain developers might develop popular metaverse-like applications with more organic users than a large tech giant.

Closing thoughts

While a single, united metaverse is likely a long way off, we already can see developments that may lead to its creation. It looks to be yet another sci-fi use case for blockchain technology and cryptocurrencies. If we will ever really reach the point of a metaverse is unsure. But in the meantime, we can already experience metaverse-like projects and continue to integrate blockchain more into our daily lives.

Printed by Libri Plureos GmbH in Hamburg,
Germany